MANCHESTER

Wit & Humour

MORRIS E. SINGER

BRADWELL
BOOKS

Published by Bradwell Books
9 Orgreave Close Sheffield S13 9NP
Email: books@bradwellbooks.co.uk
Compiled by Morris E Singer

British Library Cataloguing in Publication Data: a catalogue record for
this book is available from the British Library.

1st Edition

ISBN: 9781909914421

Print: Gomer Press, Llandysul, Ceredigion SA44 4JL
Design by: jenksdesign@yahoo.co.uk/07506 471162
Illustrations: ©Tim O'Brien 2014

A man from Eccles went to sign on at the job centre. The man there said "I've got just the job for you. Can you drive?"

"I can", said the Eccles man.

"Well", said the job centre assistant "Start tomorrow, driver/conductor on a city centre bus. That means you drive as well as collecting fares."

So the next day, the man got on the road with his double-decker bus. At about three in the afternoon the phone rang in the bus depot. The man was on the phone, "Can you get here quickly? The bus has gone through a shop window, broken glass everywhere."

"Oh no!" said the inspector on the other end, "How did it happen?"

"I don't know," said the driver "I was upstairs taking the fares at the time!"

What do you call a Mancunian in a bank?

Safe!

Two blokes from Bury went into a pub.

The first man said "A pint o' bitter, and a half o' shandy for my mate 'Donkey', please!"

The publican replied "What's with him calling you 'Donkey'?"

The second one said "Oh, 'e aw, 'e aw, 'e always calls me that!"

What do you call a Mancunian in a filing cabinet?

Sorted!

A strong young man working on a busy Manchester construction site was bragging that he could outdo anyone in a feat of strength. He made a special case of making fun of Morris, one of the older workmen. After several minutes, Morris had had enough.

"Why don't you put your money where your mouth is?' he said. 'I will bet a week's wages that I can haul something in a wheelbarrow over to that outbuilding that you won't be able to wheel back."

"You're on, old man," the boaster replied. "It's a bet! Let's see what you got."

Morris reached out and grabbed the wheelbarrow by the handles. Then, nodding to the young man, he said, "All right. Get in."

A general was troops in Hampshire and ordered the parade to put on gas masks. He paused opposite a soldier from Manchester. Pointing to the eyepiece of his respirator, he enquired: "Soldier, where is your anti-mist?".

"Don't know, Sir" came the reply "Think she's oop with Uncle Albert in Oldham".

A man from Chadderton once bought two horses, but soon realised that he couldn't tell them apart. So he asked the farmer who lived next door what he should do. The farmer suggested he measure them.

The man came back triumphantly and said: "The white horse is two inches taller than the black horse!".

Did you hear about the truck driver from Prestwich who was seen desperately chiselling away at the brickwork after his lorry got stuck while passing through a tunnel?

"Why don't you let some air out of your tyres?" asked a helpful passer-by.

"No, mate," replied the driver "It's the roof that won't go under, not the wheels."

A family from Tameside went on holiday to Benidorm. One day they went out for dinner and ordered a meal. The father of the family thought that his pie needed some gravy and shouted over to the waiter "'Ast tha Bisto fort pah?". The waiter replied in a southern English accent, "I'm sorry, mate, I don't speak Spanish."

The Beatles wrote a song about Wigan.... It's called Wigan work it out!

One day, two women got chatting while waiting for their respective flights at Heathrow Airport.

The first woman was from London and married to a wealthy man.

The second was a well mannered elderly woman from Bolton.

When the conversation moved to whether they had any children, the London woman started by saying, "When my first child was born, my husband built a beautiful mansion for me."

The woman from Bolton commented, "Well, bless your heart."

The first woman continued, "When my second child was born,

my husband bought me a beautiful vintage car."

Again, the woman from Bolton commented, "Well, bless your heart."

The first woman continued boasting, "Then, when my third child was born, my husband bought me this exquisite diamond bracelet."

Yet again, the Bolton woman commented, "Well, bless your heart."

The first woman then asked her new friend, "What did your husband buy for you when you had your first child?"

"My husband sent me to charm school," said the Mancunian lady.

"Charm school?" the first woman cried, "Oh, my goodness! What on earth for?"

The Mancunian responded, "Well for example, instead of saying, "Who cares?" I learned to say, "Well, bless your heart."

What is a Wigan kebab?

Four meat pies on a brush steel... (A brush steel is local dialect for broom handle...)

One summer evening during a violent thunderstorm in Stockport, a mother was tucking her small boy into bed. She was about to turn off the light when he asked in a nervous voice, "Mummy, will you sleep in my room tonight?" The mother smiled and gave him a reassuring hug. "I can't dear," she said. "I have to sleep in Daddy's room."

A long silence was broken at last by a shaken little voice saying, "The big sissy."

A man from Liverpool, roused by a Mancunian's scorn of his kind, protested that he was born a Scouser and hoped to die a Scouser. "Mate," scoffed the Mancunian, "Have you no ambition?".

Unusual place and street names

Affetside, near Bury

Bottoms Fold, Mossley, Ashton under Lyme

Diggle, East of Oldham

Dukinfield, Tameside

Grotton, Oldham

Ramsbottom, north of Bury

Wham Bottom Lane, Healey

Two Londoners were walking around Bolton when they stopped at a shop and looked in the window. One said to the other, "Look! Shirts £1, quilts £1.50, sheets 50p. It's so cheap here, I'm going to buy loads and sell them when we get back home." So in he walked in and asked to buy 20 shirts, quilts and sheets. The woman at the counter said "You're not from Bolton, are you?" to which he replied "How did you know?" The woman answered "This is a dry cleaner's."

One Manchester woman said to another "Hi, did you have a good Summer at home in Oldham?"

The other one replied "Yes indeed, we had a great picnic that afternoon!"

A Manchester United fan walked into a pub popular with Manchester City fans and said "Who wants to hear a joke about City?" A big bloke got up and said: "Listen, man, I'm 6 foot 3, weighing in at 90 kilos." Then he pointed at the man in the City shirt to his left. "And my friend here is 6 foot 6 and weighs in at more than 100 kilos." And, pointing to another tall man in full Manchester City outfit, he adds: "That bloke over there named Rob is a former youth boxing champion. See, you're outnumbered, three against one. So, do you still want to tell you joke?" The United fan answered: "Well, no. Because I don't like to explain the same joke three times…"

At a pub in Urmston, a special act had been put on to entertain the regulars, a magician. Being traditional, he was pulling coins out of ears, matches out of matchboxes and so on. At the end of his act, he said to one elderly regular, "Did you enjoy my act then?" "I certainly did, mate!" said the man. The magician replied "Would you be surprised if I put my hand in your jacket pocket and pulled a rabbit out?" "I would an' all" said the regular. "I've got a ferret in there!"

You know you're a Mancunian when...

Your dog wears boots too.

Three Wigan Athletic fans and three Bolton Wanderers fans were going on day trip by train. At the train station, the three Wigan supporters each bought their tickets and watched in confusion as the three Bolton fans bought just one ticket between them. "How are three people going to travel on only one ticket?" asked one of the Wigan group. "Watch this!" answered one of the Bolton supporters.

The group got onto the train. But while the Wigan fans sat in their seats, all three of the Bolton group crowded into the train toilet and closed the door behind them.

Shortly after the train left, the conductor came round to check tickets. He knocked on the toilet door and said, "Ticket, please!" The door opened a fraction and a single arm emerged with a ticket in hand. The conductor took it, checked it and moved on. The Wigan fans watched all this and agreed it was quite a clever idea. So, on the return trip, they decided to copy the Bolton fans on the return trip and save some money. When they got to the station, they bought a single ticket for the return trip. To their astonishment, the Bolton group didn't buy a ticket at all. "How are you going to travel without a ticket?" asks one perplexed Wigan follower. "Watch" said one of them.

When they got onto the train, the three Wigan fans all crammed together into a toilet and the three Bolton fans squished into another one nearby. The train started up. Shortly afterwards, one of the Bolton group left the toilet and walked over to the toilet in which the Wigan fans were hiding. He knocked on the door and said, "Ticket, please."

At a big match, a big group of Rochdale supporters, unable to get tickets, stood outside the stadium shouting up at Oldham Athletic supporters for updates on the state of play. Suddenly there was a massive roar from the crowd, so the Rochdale fans outside shouted up, "What's happening? What's happening?" The Oldham supporters shouted back, "All the Rochdale team have been carried off injured. There's only one player left on the field". Ten minutes passed. Then there was another massive roar from the crowd. The Oldham Athletic supporters shouted up "What's happening? Our player scored, has he?"

Why did the book join the police?

He wanted to go undercover!

A visitor to Rochdale arrived on a rainy day. She got up the next day and it was raining. It also rained the day after that…and the day after that. She went out to lunch and saw a little boy. In her fed up state, she asked, "Hey. Does it ever stop raining around here?"

The boy replied, "How should I know? I'm only six."

Why were the Liverpool players late for their next big match?

They were stuck on a broken escalator!

A man went to the doctor one day and said: "I've just been playing football and when I got back, I found that when I touched my legs, my arms, my head and everywhere else, it really hurt."

After a thorough examination the doctor said: "You've broken your finger."

How many Liverpool fans does it take to change a light bulb?

None, they're all happy living in Manchester United's shadow!

Supporters waiting to watch the latest Man U vs. Liverpool match heard that the Liverpool players were going to be delayed.

The team had passed a sign on the motorway that said 'Clean Lavatories'...so they did.

A priest was having a well deserved day off by the seaside at Blackpool when he saw two Manchester United supporters out in a boat. Suddenly he noticed in the water that a Liverpool fan was being attacked by a shark. Fortunately, a boat arrived and the United fans pulled the Liverpool supporter into the boat to safety, killed the shark and pulled it onto the boat.

The priest beckoned the boat to the shore and said "I've never seen anything so brave. I understood that there was intense rivalry between Manchester United fans and Liverpool fans but that has restored my faith in mankind". He then blessed the men and left.

One of the men turned to his friend and asked "What was he on about?"

"Dunno" said his mate "But he knows sod all about shark fishing. Do we need any fresh bait?"

When Chris moved to London, he constantly annoyed his new acquaintances by boasting about how great his home region of Greater Manchester was.

Finally, in exasperation, one said, "If Manchester is so wonderful, how come you didn't stay there?" "Well," answered Chris, "They're all so clever up there that I had to come down here to have any chance of making it at all."

You know you're a Mancunian when...

You know the four seasons - winter, still winter, not winter and almost winter.

At a well established manufacturing business in Droylsden, the young boss had the sad responsibility of telling one of the workers, Joe, that it was time for him to retire after 60 years with the company.

The old man was outraged:

"So, it's come to this, has it? I'm not wanted any longer?" he protested.

"I worked for your father, your grandfather and his dad too.

I tell you what, young man, if I'd known that this job wasn't going to be permanent, I would never have taken it on."

One day a United fan arrived at Old Trafford for a big match. He was a little late and the match soon kicked off. The fan was surprised to notice that the seat next to him was still empty. He asked the man on the other side of the empty seat if the person was with him.

"No." answered the man, "It's my wife's seat but she died suddenly."

"Oh I'm so sorry, mate," said the other man"...couldn't you have given it to a friend or relative or something?"

"I would have done" said the other man, "But they've all gone to the funeral."

A man from Stalybridge was walking slowly home one evening, taking his time after a heavy night at the pub with his friends.

He suddenly noticed a man from the water board with a big 'T' handle, in the middle of the road opening a valve at the bottom of a manhole.

He walked up behind him and gave him a shove.

"What was that for?" asked the startled man.

The drunken man replied, "That's for turning all the streets round when I'm trying to find my way home!"

Have you heard about the latest machine in the Arndale Centre Amusement arcade?

You put ten pence in and ask it any question and it gives you a true answer.

One holiday maker from down south tried it.

He asked the machine "Where is my father?" The machine replied:

"Your father is fishing in Bognor Regis."

Well, he thought, that's daft for a start because my father is dead.

"Where is my mother's husband?"

Back came the reply, "Your mother's husband is buried in Croyden, but your father is still fishing in Bognor Regis."

A man from Denton was building a garden shed and he ran out of nails so he went to the hardware store to buy some more. "How long do you want them?" asked the assistant. "Oh, I need to keep them," replied the man.

It was a quiet night in Horwich and a man and his wife were tucked up in bed fast asleep when there was an unexpected knock on the door. The man looked at his clock and saw that it was half past three in the morning. "I'm not getting out of bed at this time of the night," he thought, and rolled over.

A louder knock followed. "Aren't you going to answer that?" asked his wife sleepily.

So the man dragged himself out of bed and went downstairs. He opened the door and saw that there was a strange man standing at the door. It didn't take the homeowner long to realise that the man was drunk.

"Hi there," slurred the stranger. "Can you give me a push?"
"No, I'm sorry. It's half past three. I was in bed," said the man and slammed the door. He went back up to bed and told his wife what happened.

"That wasn't very nice of you," she said.

"Remember that night we broke down in the pouring rain on the way to pick the kids up from the babysitter, and you had to knock on that man's door to get us started again? What would have happened if he'd told us to get lost?"

"But the man who just knocked on our door was drunk," replied her husband.

"Well we can at least help move his car somewhere safe and sort him out a taxi," said his wife. "He needs our help." So the husband got out of bed again, got dressed, and went downstairs. He opened the door, but couldn't to see the stranger anywhere so he shouted, "Hey, do you still want a push?" In answer, he heard a voice call out, "Yes please!" So, still being unable to see the stranger, he shouted, "Where are you?"

"I'm over here," the stranger replied, "on your swing."

Pete and Larry hadn't seen each other in many years. They were having a long chat, telling each other all about their lives. Finally Pete invited Larry to visit him in his new apartment in Salford Quays. "I have a wife and three kids and I'd love to have you visit us."

"Great. Where do you live?"

"Here's the address. There's plenty of parking behind the flat. Park and come around to the front door, kick it open with your foot, go to the lift and press the button with your left elbow, then enter! When you reach the sixth floor, go down the hall until you see my name on the door. Then press the doorbell with your right elbow and I'll let you in."

"Great. But tell me...what is all this business of kicking the front door open, then pressing lift buttons with my right, then my left elbow?"

Pete answered, "Surely you're not coming empty-handed?".

At an antiques auction in Prestwich, a wealthy American announced that he had lost his wallet containing £5,000, and he would give a reward of £50 to the person who found it. From the back of the hall a local man shouted, "I'll give £100!"

A vicar from Tameside was travelling home one evening and was greatly annoyed when a young man, much the worse for drink, came and sat next to him on the bus.

"Young man," the vicar, declared in a rather pompous tone, "Do you not realise you are on the road to perdition?"

"Oh, drat and botheration," replied the drunken man, "I could have sworn this bus went to Dukinfield."

Why do Mancunians prefer mushy peas?

Because they can't keep the round ones on their knives.

A man walked up to the foreman of a road laying gang in Altrincham and asked for a job. "I haven't got one for you today." said the foreman looking up from his newspaper. "But if you walk half a mile down here, you can see if you like the work and I can put you on the list for tomorrow. "That's great mate," said the bloke as he wandered off down the road to find the gang. At the end of the shift, the man walked past the foreman and shouted, "Thanks mate. See you tomorrow." The foreman looked up from his paper and shouted back, "You've enjoyed yourself then?". "Yes I have!" shouted back the bloke, "But can I have a shovel or a pick to lean on like the rest of the gang?"

A visitor from outside the area was driving around Tyldesley in his fancy new car and found that he was lost. The driver stopped old Jim and said, "You there! Old man, what happens if I turn left here?" "Don't know sir," replied old Jim.

"Well what if I turn right here, where will that take me?" continued the visitor. "Don't know sir." replied Jim. Becoming exasperated, the driver continued, "Well, what if I go straight on?" A flicker of knowledge moved over old Jim's face until he replied, "Don't know sir." "I say old man you don't know a lot do you?" retorted the posh bloke. Jim looked at him and said, "I may not know a lot but I ain't lost like you are!" With that, old Jim walked off leaving the motorist stranded.

Robert proudly drove his new convertible into Stockport town centre with his shiny new footspa resting in the back seat.

He had walked half way around the block from the parked car when he realised that the sunny weather had caused him to leave the hood down... with his footspa in the back.

He ran all the way back to his car, but it was too late... Another five footspas had been dumped in the car.

A passenger in a taxi travelling through Middleton tapped the driver on the shoulder to ask him something. The driver screamed, lost control of the cab, nearly hit a bus, drove up over the curb and stopped just inches from a large plate glass window.

For a few moments everything was silent in the cab, then the driver said, "Please, don't ever do that again. You scared the daylights out of me."

The passenger, who was also frightened, apologised and said he didn't realise that a tap on the shoulder could frighten him so much, to which the driver replied, "I'm sorry, it's really not your fault at all. Today is my first day driving a cab. I've been driving a hearse for the last 25 years."

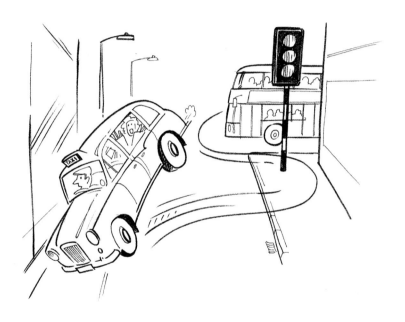

A man from Sale phoned his son in London three days before Christmas and said, "I hate to ruin your day but I have to tell you that your mother and I are divorcing; forty-five years of misery is enough."

"Dad, what are you talking about?" his son shouted

"We can't stand the sight of each other any longer" his father said, 'We're sick of each other and I'm sick of talking about this, so you call your sister in Manchester and tell her."

Frantic, the son called his sister, who yelled "Like hell they're getting divorced!" she shouted, "I'll take care of this!"

She immediately called her father and yelled at him 'You are not getting divorced. Don't do a single thing until I get there.

I'm calling my brother back, and we'll both be there tomorrow. Until then, don't do a thing, DO YOU HEAR ME?".

Then she hung up.

The old man hung up his phone and turned to his wife. "Sorted! They're coming for Christmas - and they're paying their own way."

A Worsley man fell out with his in-laws and banned them from entering the house while he was in it. His wife faithfully carried out his wishes until she was on her death bed and then asked sadly, "Haven't I always been a supportive wife to you, John?" "Yes my dear." He replied "The best". "Then I would love it if you could grant my last request and let my sister Sarah ride in the first car with you at my funeral?" "Alright, my dear" he agreed heavily, "But I'm warning you, it'll spoil all my pleasure!"

A father and his son, Bobby, arrived at the big match at the Etihad Stadium and Dad suddenly realised that he couldn't find their tickets. He said to his son, "Nip home and see if I left the tickets there." Bobby replied "No probs, Dad." Half an hour later Bobby returned to his dad who was patiently waiting outside the football pitch. He said to his dad, "Yep, they're on the kitchen table where you left them."

Jim was having a pint in the Holts Arms one night when in walked Simon, a very brash man from London. Jim couldn't help overhearing Simon trying to encourage some people to bet that they couldn't drink 20 pints in 20 minutes. Despite a great deal of persuasion, Simon was still failing in his attempt to make some money. Then he looked at Jim and said "Well what about you then? Are you interested?" Jim quickly drank the rest of his pint and left the pub.

Half an hour later, Jim walked back into the pub and said to Simon "OK, I'll take that bet."

Simon was delighted at the thought of winning the bet. But his excitement soon faded when Jim drank down the 20 pints in 19 minutes. Handing over the money, Simon said "When you left here earlier, where did you go?" Jim looked at him and replied "I had to go to pub down the road to see if I could do it first."

A Liverpool fan was once walking through the desert when he stumbled across an old lamp. He picked it up and rubbed it and a genie appeared before his eyes.

"You have two wishes," said the genie "Use them wisely."

So the Liverpool fan said "I want an everlasting pie!"

The genie gave him a pie. The Liverpool supporter ate a bit of it and then said "Mmm that's good.

"And your second wish?" asked the genie. – "I'll have another one of these." Came the reply.

A boy from Farnworth was getting ready to start his new school term. Because he was getting older and more independent, his father gave him £2 for him to catch the bus home. But instead of getting on the bus, the boy ran behind it all the way home. His father came home and the boy proudly said, "Dad, I saved you £2 today because I ran behind the bus instead of getting on!" The man stormed out of the room, shouting "You should have run behind a taxi and saved me 40 quid you little..."

A man went into a hardware store and asked to buy a sink. "Would you like one with a plug?" asked the assistant. "Don't tell me they've gone electric!" said the man.

A Liverpudlian man was going for a job interview in Bury and on the way there, he asked a local man for directions:

"Excuse me mate could you possibly tell me the quickest way to Bury town centre?"

The man replied, "You driving or walking, lad?"

The Bury man replied, "Driving."

The Liverpudlian nodded, saying, "Yup, definitely the quickest way"

Johnny was down on his luck so he thought he would try getting a few odd jobs by calling at the big houses in Altrincham. After a few rejections, a man in one of the big houses thought he would give him a chance so he said "The porch needs painting so I'll give you £50 to paint it for me."

"That's great. You're a life saver. I'll get started straight away!" said the man

His one-off employer handed him a paintbrush and a tin of cream paint.

Time passed and the man came back, knocked on the door and said "There you go. It's all done! Painting completed and finished."

"Great. Here's you £50"

"Thanks very much. Oh by the way, it's a Ferrari, not a Porsche!"

Three friends, one from Manchester University, one from University of London and one from the Liverpool University, were out having a good time together at a funfair. They were just about to go on the helter-skelter when an old woman stepped in front of them.

"This is a magic ride," she said. "You will land in whatever you shout out on the way down."

"I'm up for this," said the Manchester student and slid down the helter-skelter shouting "GOLD!" at the top of his voice. Sure enough, when he hit the bottom he found himself surrounded by thousands of pounds worth of gold coins. The London student went next and shouted "SILVER!" at the top of his voice. At the bottom he landed in more silver coinage than he could carry.

The Liverpool student went last and, launching himself from the top of the slide shouted "WEEEEEEE!".

A lawyer from Liverpool and a businessman from Altrincham from ended up sitting next to each other on a flight to airport.

The lawyer started thinking that he could have some fun at his fellow passenger's expense and asked him if he'd like to play a fun game. The businessman was tired and just wanted to relax. He politely declined the offer and tried to sleep. The lawyer man persisted, explaining:

"I ask you a question, and if you don't know the answer, you pay me only £5; you ask me one, and if I don't know the answer, I will pay you £500."

This got the other man a little more interested and he finally agreed to play the game.

The lawyer man asked the first question, "What's the distance from the Earth to the moon?"

The businessman said nothing, but reached into his pocket, pulled out a five-pound note and handed it to the other man.

Now, it was the other chap's turn. He asked the lawyer, "What goes up a hill with three legs, and comes down with four?"

The lawyer used his laptop. He used the air-phone; he searched the web, he sent emails to his most well read friends, but still came up with nothing. After an hour of searching, he finally gave up.

He woke up the other man and handed him £500. The man smugly pocketed the cash and went straight back to sleep.

The lawyer man went wild with curiosity wanting to know the answer. He woke the businessman up and asked, "Well? What goes up a hill with three legs and comes down with four?"

The businessman reached into his pocket, handed the other man £5 and went back to sleep.

A man was rushing to a hospital from a business trip because his wife had just gone into labour with twins, and there was a strange family tradition that the first family member to arrive got to name the children. The man was afraid that his wayward brother would show up first and give his kids awful names. When he finally arrived at the hospital in a cold sweat he saw his brother sitting in the waiting room, waving, with a silly grin on his face. He walked unhappily in to see his wife who was scowling and holding two little babies, a boy and a girl. Almost afraid to hear it, the man asked, "What did he name the girl?" "Denise" says the wife. "Hey that's not too bad! What did he name the boy?" "De-nephew."

A man was sitting in a cafe in Bury, he was fed up and had come out for a bit of company and to try and cheer him-self up. He picked up the menu and noticed that it only featured three dishes: meatloaf, shepherd's pie and Bury black pudding. The waitress came over to take his order. "I'll have the Bury black pudding," said the man glumly, "and if you could throw in a few kind words that would be very welcome." The waitress left and returned a few minutes later with a plate of Bury black pudding. She banged the plate on the table in front of the man and started to walk off. "Hey," said the man. "I got my dinner; how about those kind words?" The waitress turned, paused and said, "Don't eat the Bury black pudding."

A dog ran into a butcher's shop in Chadderton and grabbed some sirloin steak off the counter. But the butcher recognized the dog as belonging to a neighbour of his who happened to be a lawyer. The butcher called up his neighbour and said, "If your dog stole steak from my butcher shop, would you be liable for the cost of the meat?" The lawyer replied, "Of course, how much was the sirloin?" The butcher replied "Seven pounds." A few days later the butcher received a cheque for seven pounds - and an invoice stating "Legal Consultation Service: £150."

Why did the lazy man want a job in a bakery?
So he could loaf around!

A labourer shouted up to his roofer mate on top of an old house in Hyde, saying, "Don't start climbing down this ladder, Burt." "Why not?" Burt called back. "Cos I moved it five minutes ago!" replied his mate.

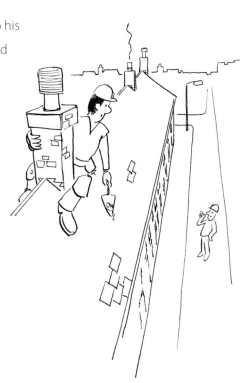

One day a man walked into a bar in Audenshaw and ordered a beer. He took his first sip and put it down. While he was looking around the bar, a monkey leapt down and stole the pint of beer so swiftly that there was nothing he could do. The man asked who owned the thieving little monkey and the barman pointed to the bloke playing the piano. The man walked over and says "Oi - do you know your monkey just stole my blooming beer?" The pianist replied "No, but if you hum it, I'll play it."

A man made a phone call and asked "What time does the Central Library open?"

"Nine am" came the reply. "And what's the idea of calling me at home in the middle of the night to ask a question like that?"

"Not until nine am?" came the plaintive reply.

"No, not till nine am!" the librarian replied. "Why do you want to get in before nine am?

"Who said I wanted to get in?" the man sighed sadly. "I want to get out."

A couple from Radcliffe both retired at the same time. The husband had always had a dream about being able to play the piano, so his wife bought him a piano for his birthday. A few weeks later, her friend asked how he was getting on with it. "Oh, we returned the piano." said the other woman, "I persuaded him to switch to a clarinet instead."

"Why's that?" asked her friend "Because," she answered, "with a clarinet, he can't sing."

A man travelling him from a business trip found himself sitting next to a chatty woman on the plane. "Hi there! My name is Alice," said the old lady. "It's so nice to meet you! I'm flying to New York for my grandson's fifth birthday. I'm so excited! I remember when he was just a little baby and now he's already five! It's really hard to believe. He's the most adorable thing you've ever seen! You know what? Hold on, I think I might have a picture on me. Let me take a look in my purse, yes, here it is, just look at him, isn't he adorable. Do you see his dimple on his left cheek? Simply adorable! I could stare at his picture all day. Oh my, and you should hear him on the phone! He is just the cutest, he says to me in the cutest voice "Hi Grandma!" It just gets me all teary eyed."

After what seemed like two hours for the poor man sitting next to her, Alice seemed to realize that perhaps she was talking a bit too much. "You know, I feel terrible! Here I am just talking and talking without letting you get in a word edgeways! Tell me, what do you think about my Grandson?

One day a man went into a bank in Salford, asking for a £2000 loan. "Well, before we lend you the money we're going to need some kind of security" the bank clerk said. "No problem" the man responded "Here are the keys to my car "You'll see it, it's a red Ferrari parked in the back of your car park." A few weeks, later the man returned to pay off his loan. While he was paying it up, along with the interest of £10, the manager came over, "Sir, we're delighted to have your business, but if you don't mind me asking, after you left we looked into you and found out that you are a millionaire. Why would you need to borrow £2000 from the bank?"

"Well," the man replied "It's quite simple, where else could I park my car for three weeks in Salford for £10?"

A magician was a regular part of the entertainment on a cruise ship. Because the audience was different each week, the magician performed the same tricks over and over again. The problem with this was that the captain's parrot saw the shows each week and began to understand how the magician did every trick.

Once he understood, he started shouting in the middle of the show, "Look, it's not the same hat!" or, "Look, he's hiding the flowers under the table!" Or "Hey, why are all the cards the ace of spades?"

The magician was furious, but he couldn't do anything because it was the Captain's parrot.

Then one stormy night in the middle of a cruise, the ship started to sink. Luckily all the passengers escaped unharmed on the lifeboats.

Sadly, the magician was so busy helping save others that he was left behind and found himself hanging on to a piece of wood floating in the middle of the sea…with the parrot.

They stared at each other with hatred, but did not utter a word.

This silence went on for a day…then two days. Then three days. Finally on the fourth day, the parrot could not hold back any longer and said…

"Okay, I give up. Where's the blinking ship??"

A Gorton man's dog died and as it was a favourite pet, the man decided to have a gold statue made by a jeweller to remember the dog by.

The Manchester man asked: "Can you make us a gold statue of me dog?"

Jeweller: "Do you want it 18 carat?"

"No", replied the Gorton man "I want it chewin' a bone, yer daft beggar!"

The Seven Dwarves were walking through the forest one day when they suddenly fell into a deep ravine. Snow White, who was following along behind her friends, stared over the edge of the ravine and called out to the dwarfs. From the very depths of the dark hole a voice came back, "Liverpool could win the Champions League."

Snow White heaved a sigh of relief, thinking "Well, at least Dopey's survived!"

How many Liverpool fans does it take to change a light bulb?

560,001. That is: 1 to change it, 60,000 to say they've been changing it for years and 500,000 to buy the replica kit!